WORLD'S WORST JOKES

For Diane, Dan, Tom, Simon and Jake,
and a drunken joke-fuelled night in The Groucho Club

WORLD'S WORST JOKES

Tony Husband

TED SMART

This edition published for The Book People Ltd, Hall Wood Avenue, Haydock, St Helens, WA11 0UL

First published by Ebury Press in Great Britain 2006

1 3 5 7 9 10 8 6 4 2

Text © Tony Husband 2006

Tony Husband has asserted his right to be identified as the author of this work under the Copyright, Designs and Patents Act 1988.

Ebury Press, an imprint of Ebury Publishing. Random House, 20 Vauxhall Bridge Road, London SW1V 2SA

Random House Australia (Pty) Limited, 20 Alfred Street, Milsons Point, Sydney, New South Wales 2061, Australia

Random House New Zealand Limited, 18 Poland Road, Glenfield, Auckland 10, New Zealand

Random House (Pty) Limited, Isle of Houghton, Corner Boundary Road & Carse O'Gowrie, Houghton, 2198, South Africa

The Random House Group Limited Reg. No. 954009

www.randomhouse.co.uk

A CIP catalogue record for this book is available from the British Library.

Designed by seagulls.net

ISBN 9780091912307 (from January 2007)
ISBN 009191230X

Papers used by Ebury Press are natural, recyclable products made from wood grown in sustainable forests.

Printed and bound in Singapore by Tien Wah Press

Copies are available at special rates for bulk order. Contact the sales development team on 020 7840 8487
or visit www.booksforpromotions.co.uk for more information.

It's been said I'm a crap at telling jokes. Not true; I tell crap jokes. There's a difference, as anyone reading this book of the world's worst jokes will understand. Even the greatest stand-up comedian would struggle to raise a smile from this lot. So listen up: it's not the way I tell 'em, it's what I have to tell. So don't shoot the messenger. OK …

People laughed at me when I said I was going to be a comedian. Well, they're not laughing now

An Englishman, Irishman, Welshman and Scotsman are in a bar. The English man says, 'It's St George's Day today; my son was born on St George's Day and we called him George.' The Scotsman says, 'That's strange, my son was born on St Andrew's Day and we called him Andrew.' The Welshman says, 'WOW! My son was born on St David's Day and we called him David.' The Irishman says, 'Well, my son Pancake …'

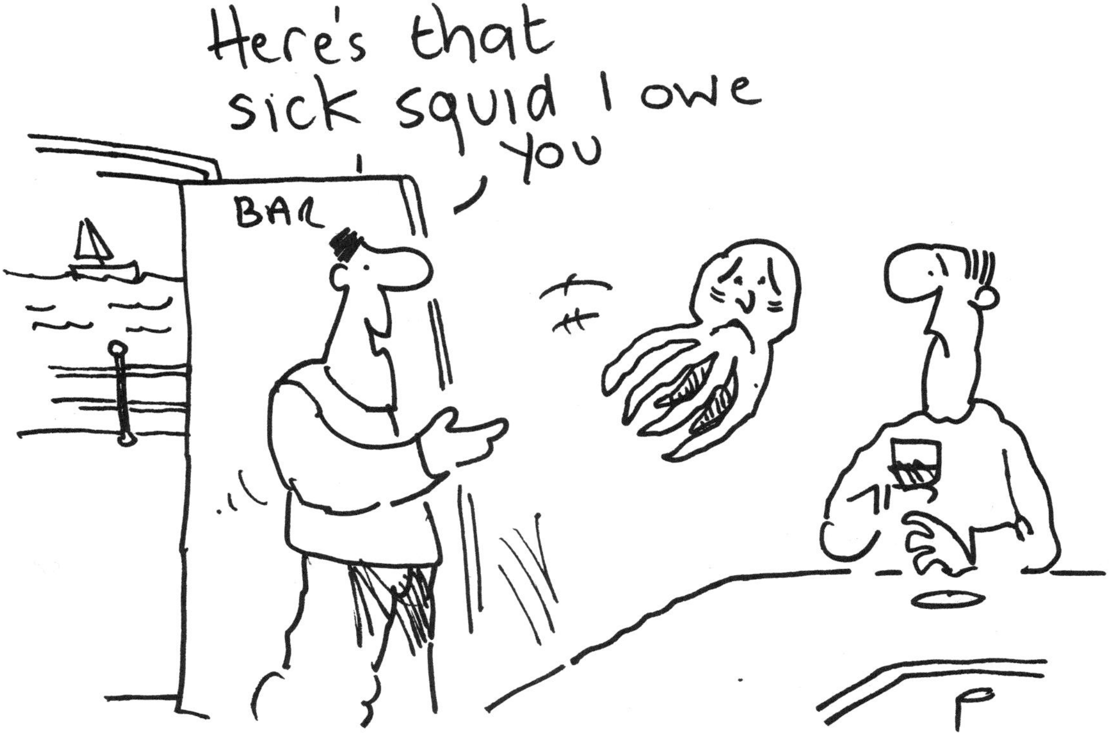
Here's that sick squid I owe you
BAR

My mates' spectacles are so thick, if you look at an A–Z, you can see people waving at you.

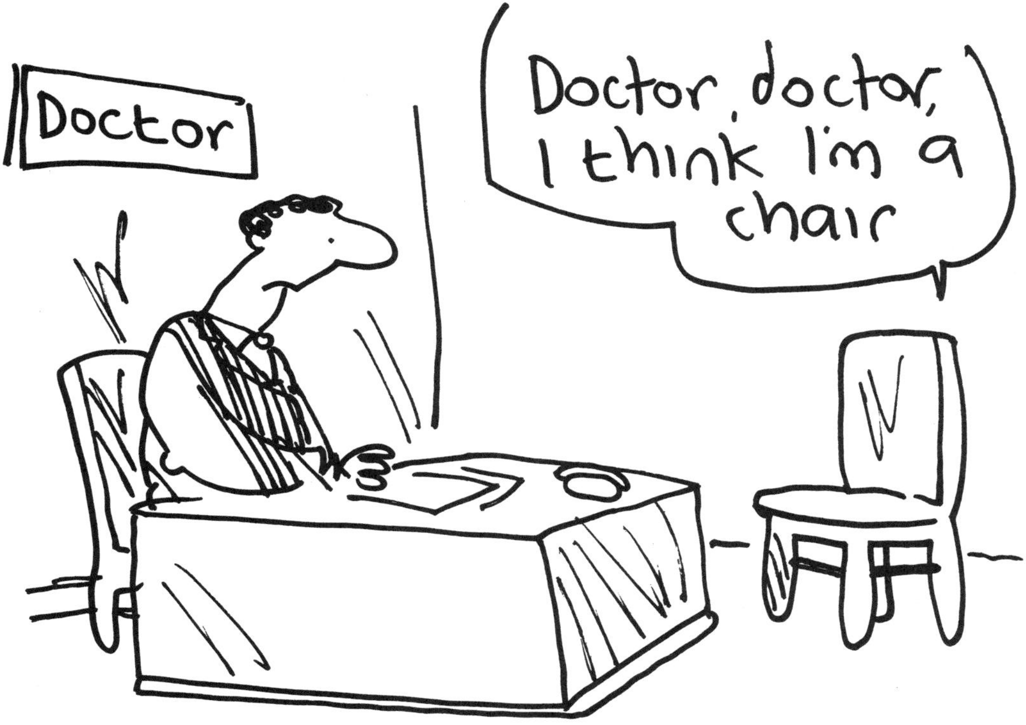
Doctor
Doctor, doctor, I think I'm a chair

My grandad's got a tattoo of England all over his body...
but at least you know where you are with him.

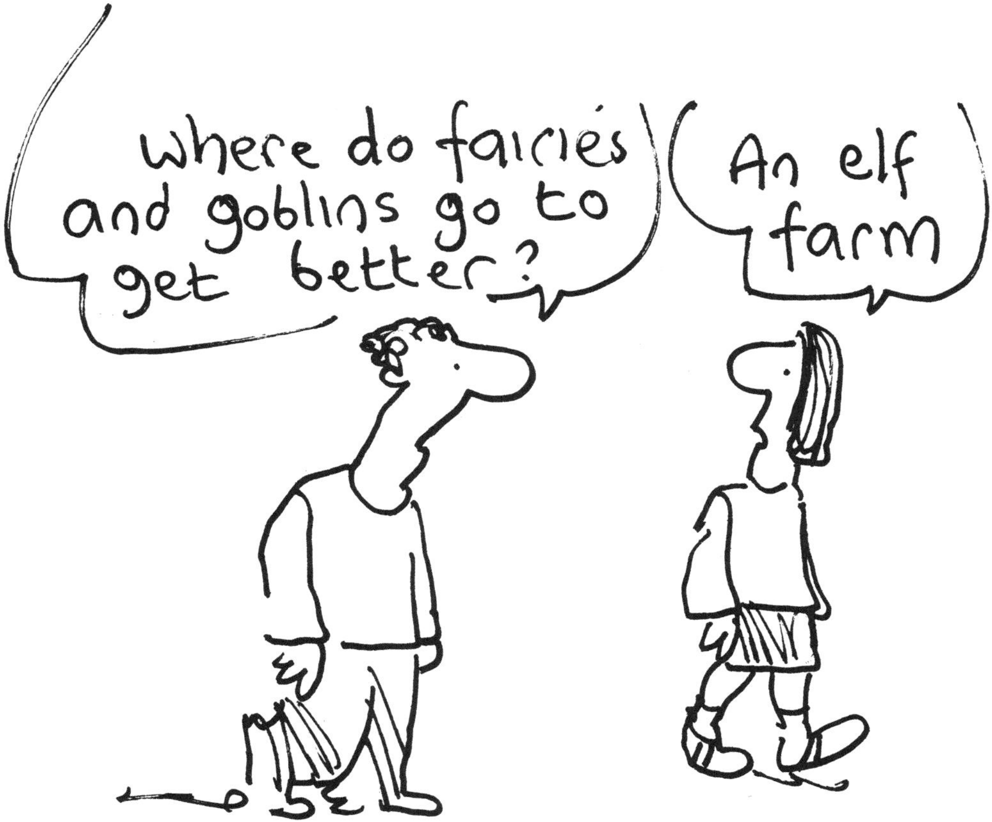
Where do fairies and goblins go to get better?
An elf farm

What's round and bad-tempered?

A vicious circle.

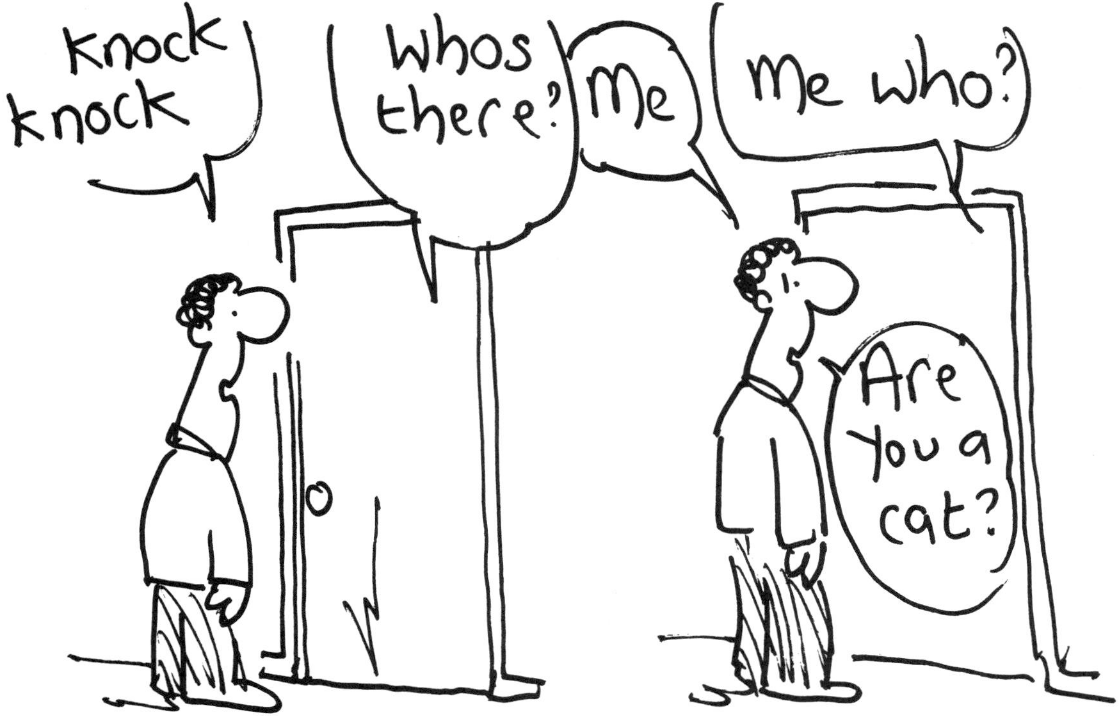
Knock knock
Whos there?
Me
Me who?
Are you a cat?

Two women are talking. 'My husband's hung like a donkey!' says one.

'The trouble is,' says the other, 'he smells like one.'

Can you recommend anything for yellow teeth?
Erm... a brown tie
CHEMIST

A woman is talking to her husband:
'If I died, would you meet someone else?'

The husband replies, 'I don't see why not.'

She says, 'Would she sleep in our bed?'

He replies, 'Probably, yeah.'

His wife asks, 'Would you play golf with her?'

He replies, 'Yeah probably'

'And would you let her use my clubs?'

Her husband replies, 'No, she's left-handed.'

Did you hear Tom Hall beat his wife to death with a 5 iron?
Really, how many strokes?

A golfer is talking to another golfer: 'This ball is brilliant! If you lose it in the rough it beeps, if you lose it in the snow it glows red, and if you hit it in the water it blows bubbles.'

'Blimey,' says his mate, 'where can I get buy one?

'I don't know,' says the golfer. 'I found it.'

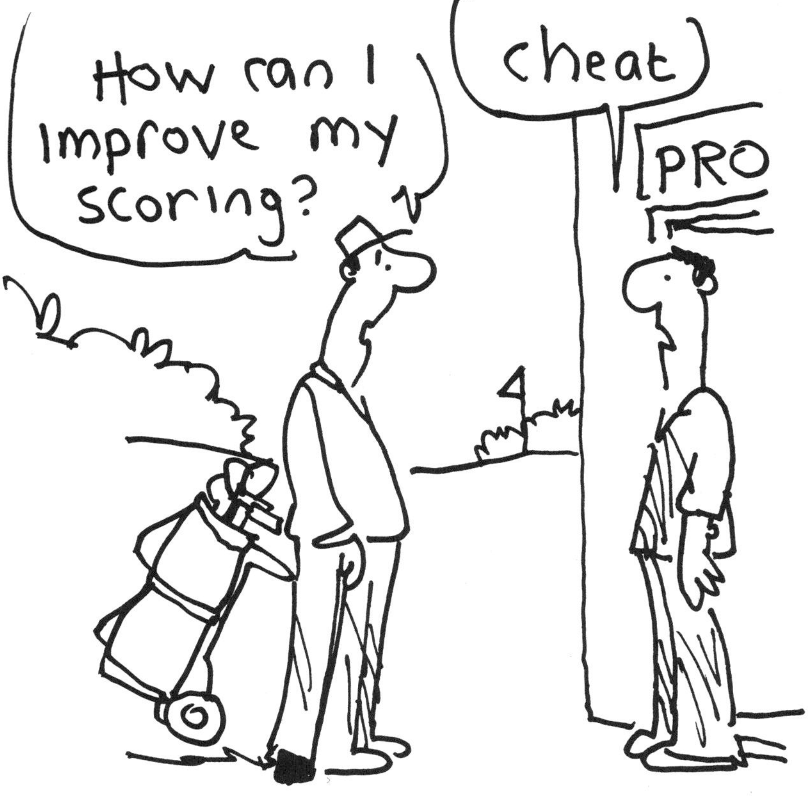
How can I improve my scoring?
cheat
PRO

Two women are looking at a baby in a pram.

The first woman says, 'Was your husband at the birth?'

The second woman says, 'No, and to be honest, he wasn't at the conception either.'

How come you're only wearing one glove? Did you lose one?
No, I found one

Secretary – Can I use your Dictaphone?

Boss – No, use your finger like everyone else.

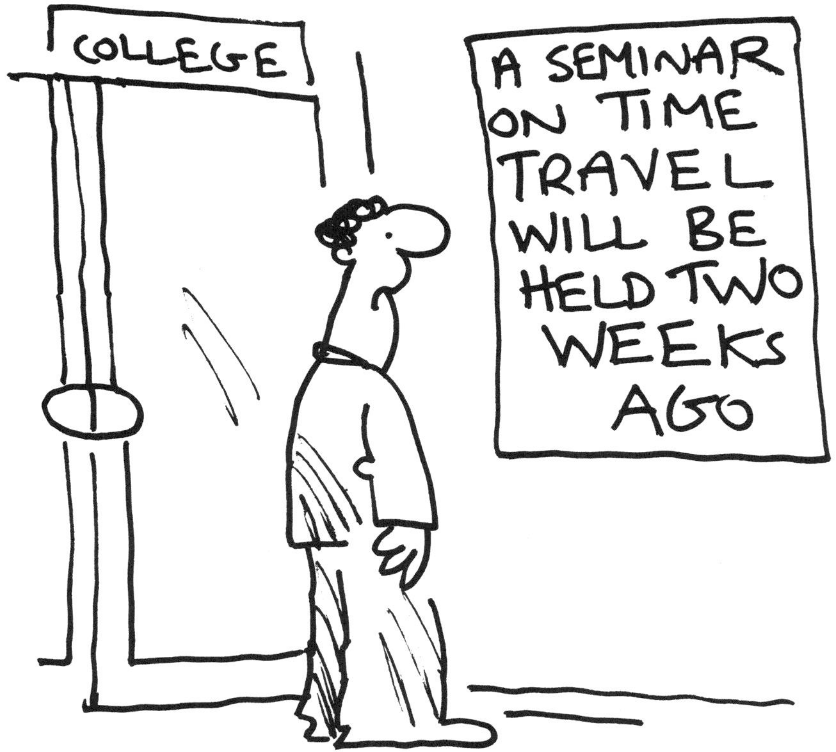
COLLEGE
A SEMINAR ON TIME TRAVEL WILL BE HELD TWO WEEKS AGO

Two blokes in a pub.

First bloke – Bill's died.

Second bloke – How?

First bloke – The big C.

Second bloke – What, he drowned?

You know, if it wasn't for electricity we'd have to watch the telly by candlelight

Who was Joan of Arc?

Answer – Noah's wife.

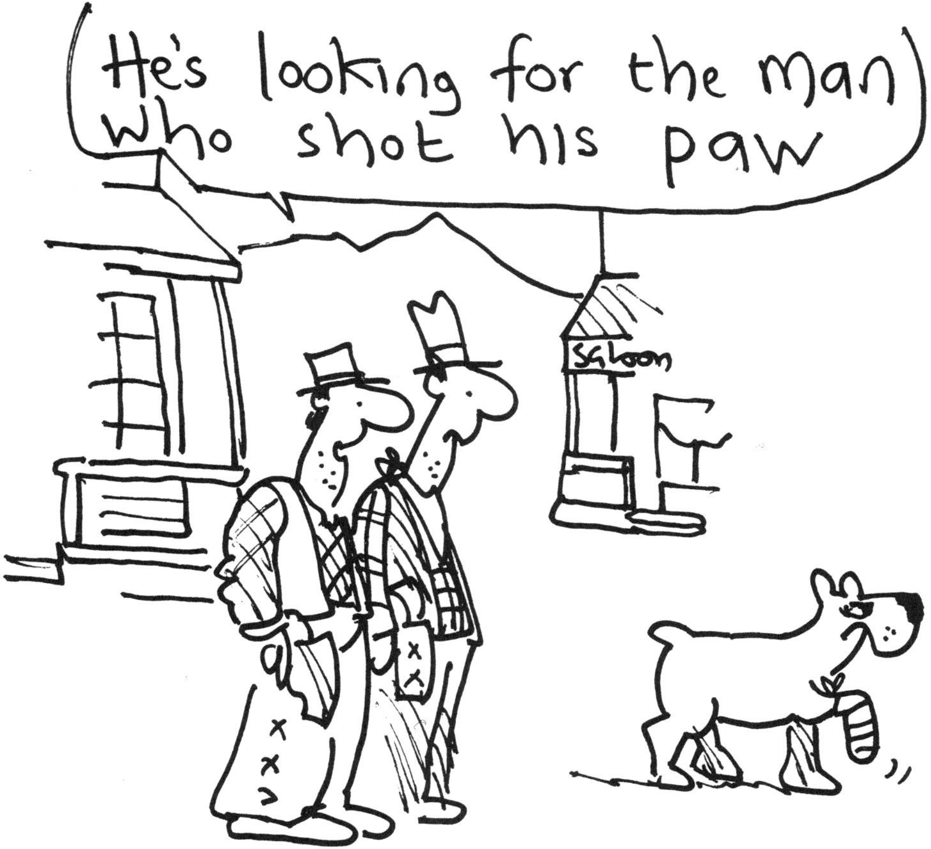
He's looking for the man who shot his paw
Saloon

What's a blizzard?

Answer – A baby buzzard.

What do you call a fly with no wings?

Answer – A walk.

shucks partner, that lion dancin' aint as much fun as I was led to believe
ZOO

Buy a microwave bed and get a good night's sleep in two minutes.

Stop pulling the cat's tail
Im not, Im holding it, it's the cat that's doing the pulling

A man goes into a bar, there are some nuts on the table and he takes a few. The nuts speak to him: 'You're a nice man, I really like you!' The man is puzzled. He walks over to the coffee machine to put some money in for a coffee. The coffee machine snaps at him: 'Piss off, you ugly bastard! Don't come anywhere near me.' The man, shocked, goes over to the bartender and tells him what happened. 'Don't worry,' says the bartender. 'The peanuts are complimentary but that coffee machine is out of order.'

How will we catch a gorilla?
Hide in a tree and make a noise like a banana

Two blokes in a pub are about to play darts. 'Nearest the bull,' says the first. 'Baa,' says the second. 'Moo,' says the first. 'Fair enough, you go first,' says the second bloke.

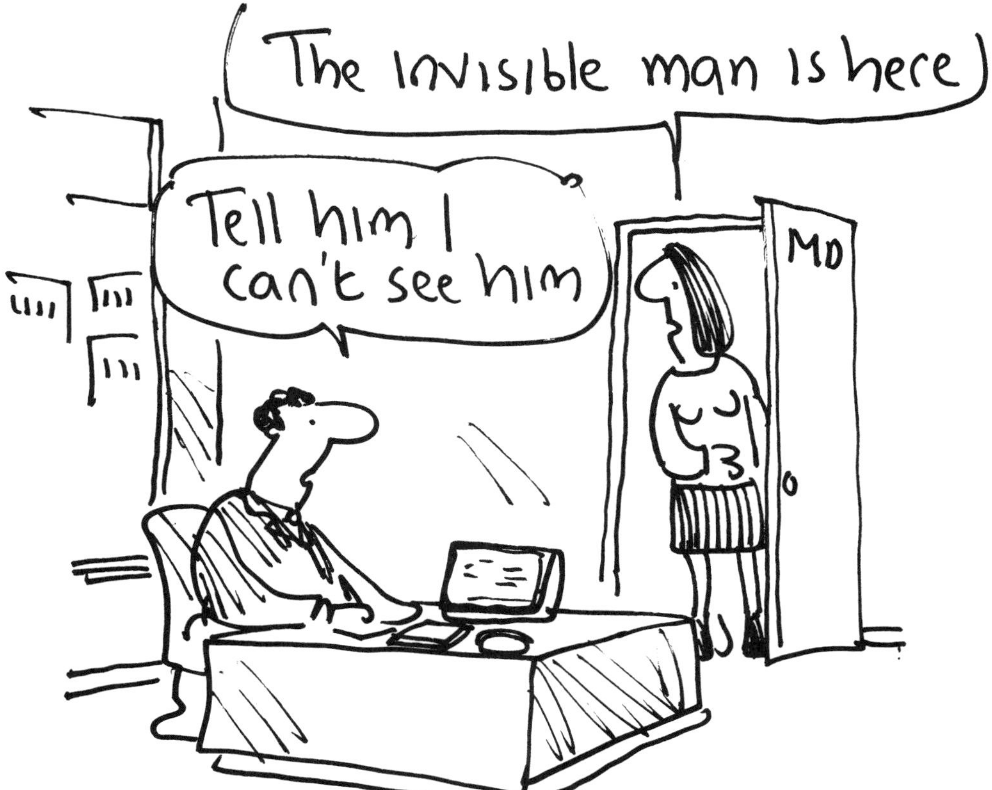
The invisible man is here
Tell him I can't see him
MD

Two ducks walking down the road.

One says, 'Quack, quack.' The other one says, 'Shut up, I can't walk any quacker!'

How shall we celebrate our 25 years of marriage?
Er... A two minute silence

Two Geordies are in the jungle.

'Are those war drums?' says one.

'No, they're ours,' says the other.

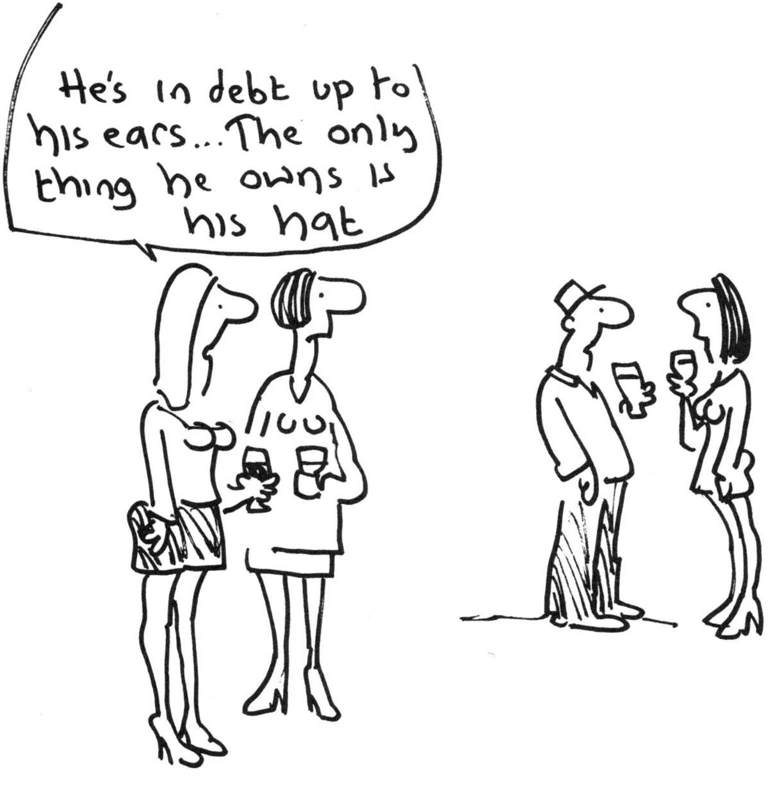
He's in debt up to his ears... The only thing he owns is his hat

Dan is at a nightclub with his mate Dave. Dan is very shy. 'I want to dance with that girl over there but I won't know what to say to her,' he says. Dave replies, 'Just be natural. Talk about anything that comes up.' So Dan goes over and starts dancing with this girl. After a while he feels the need to talk: 'You don't sweat much for a fat lass!'

My wife's a light eater, when it's light she starts eating

A man walks into the library
Pint of bitter please

Librarian
This is a library

Man in hushed tones
Sorry, pint of bitter please

I was so ugly when I was born the doctors slapped my mother

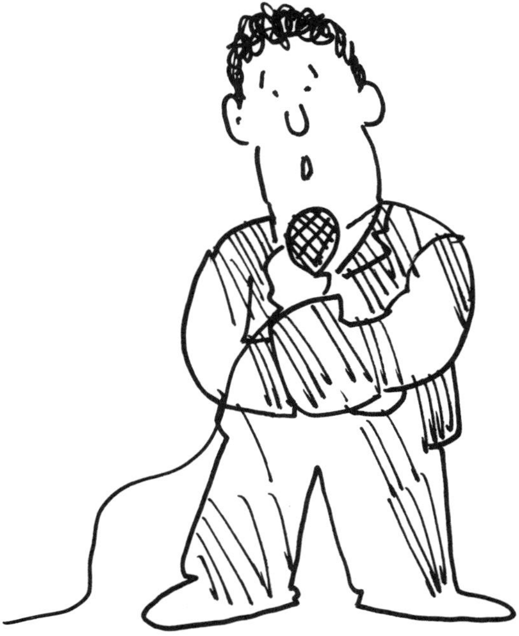

Woman – If I was your wife I'd give you poison!

The man replies – If you were my wife, I'd take it!

I met the invisible man's wife yesterday, she's invisible too
What's she like?
Not much to look at

Who's the only ice cream seller in the Bible?

Answer – Walls of Jericho.

You think you're a dog? Lie on the couch then
I'm not allowed on the couch
PSYCHIATRIST

If you ask me, speed bumps are crap.

If anything they slow you down.

How long have you thought you're a dog?
PSYCHIATRIST
Since I was a puppy

A man goes into a rare record shop and says to the owner, 'I am one of the world's leading wasp experts. Do you have any vinyl recordings of wasps?' The owner says, 'Yes but it's rare and costs thousands of pounds. I'll let you hear it.' He puts the record on the turntable and the customer snaps, 'That's not a wasp!' The owner picks the record off the turntable and looks at it. 'Sorry, I put it on the bee side.'

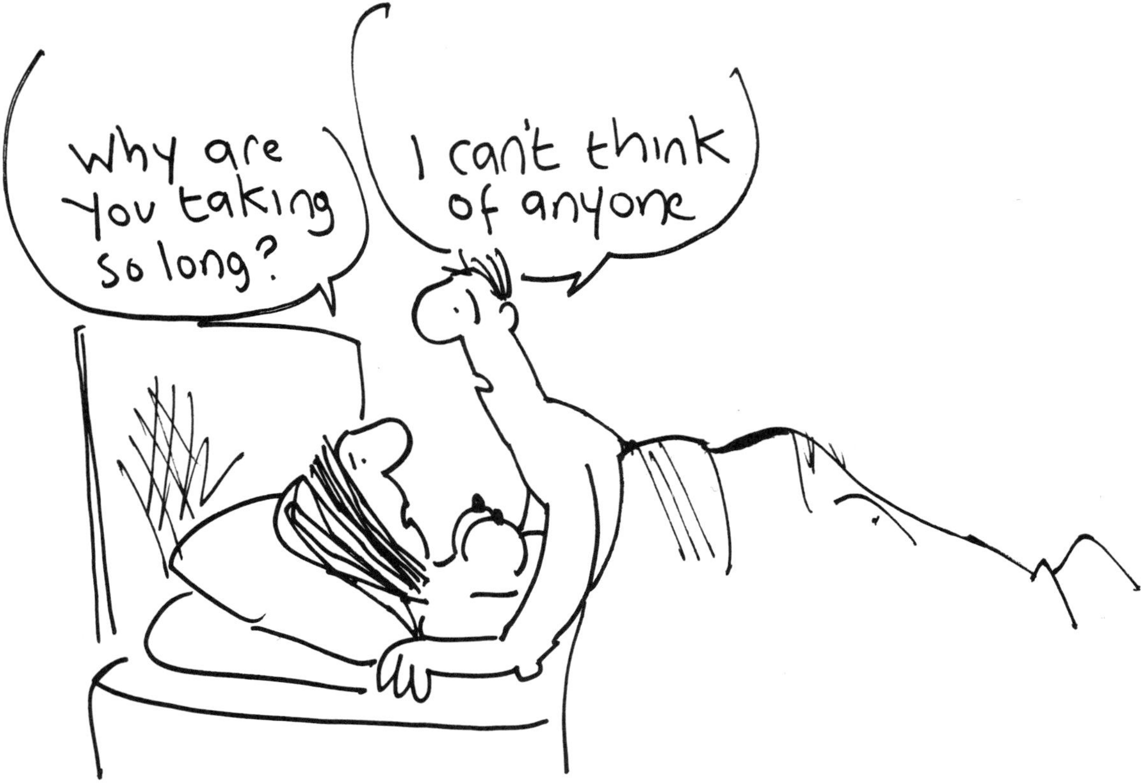
Why are you taking so long?
I can't think of anyone

A woman visiting a stately home is shown around by the guide. The woman says to the guide, 'Are there any ghosts here? Because I am absolutely petrified of them.' The guide turns to the woman and says, 'I've not seen one since I worked here.' The woman says, 'And how long have you worked here?' The guide replies, '400 years.'

The job pays £200 a week and in 6 months it goes up to £250
PERSONNEL MANAGER
OK, I'll come back in 6 months

A baby and daddy polar bear are both sitting on the glacier. The baby polar bear says, 'Daddy, am I a real polar bear?' 'Course you are, son, why do you ask?' says his dad. ''Cause my arse is bleeding freezing!'

It reads... My dear wife, I always said you'd be mentioned in my will, so: Hi Jill, I'm leaving it all to the cat
SOLICITORS
WILL

My girlfriend asked me to tease her, so I said she was fat.

I was surprised to see a painting of me in the National Portrait Gallery, then I realised it was a mirror

I went to a party recently that was so boring that when a light bulb popped we were still laughing about it two hours later.

My uncle is really mean. I went round the other day and found him stripping the wallpaper. He wasn't redecorating.... ....he was moving

I was very ugly as a child and, one day while out with my mother, a gang of kids started insulting me. My mother got really upset and sat with me on a bench outside a pub. A man came out and asked her what was wrong. She said she was just upset. So the man went in the pub and came out with a large brandy. He said to her, 'Here you are, this will cheer you up, and here's some nuts for the monkey.'

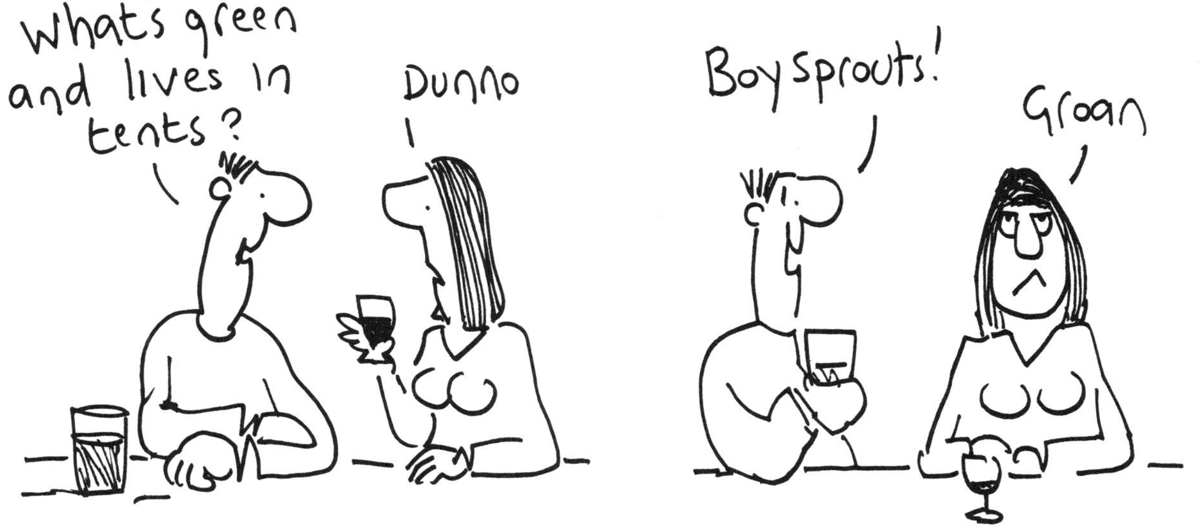
What's green and lives in tents?
Dunno
Boy sprouts!
Groan

If you cross a skunk with a koala bear you get a poo-bear.

I don't believe it. You drove the car over my bike!?
Well you shouldn't have left it on the lawn!

An Arab scientist crossed an Ostrich with a corkscrew. You give it a fright and it drills for oil.

Haven't I seen you before somewhere?
Yes, that's why I don't go there anymore!

What shakes and lives at the bottom of the sea?

Answer – A nervous wreck.

She gets her looks from her father, he's a plastic surgeon

A male panda has mated with a harmonium.
Experts believe this may create a pandemonium.

I'm sick of my dog, he chases anything on a bike
What will you do, have him put down?
No, take the bike off him

What did the shy pebble say?

Answer – I wish I was a little bolder.

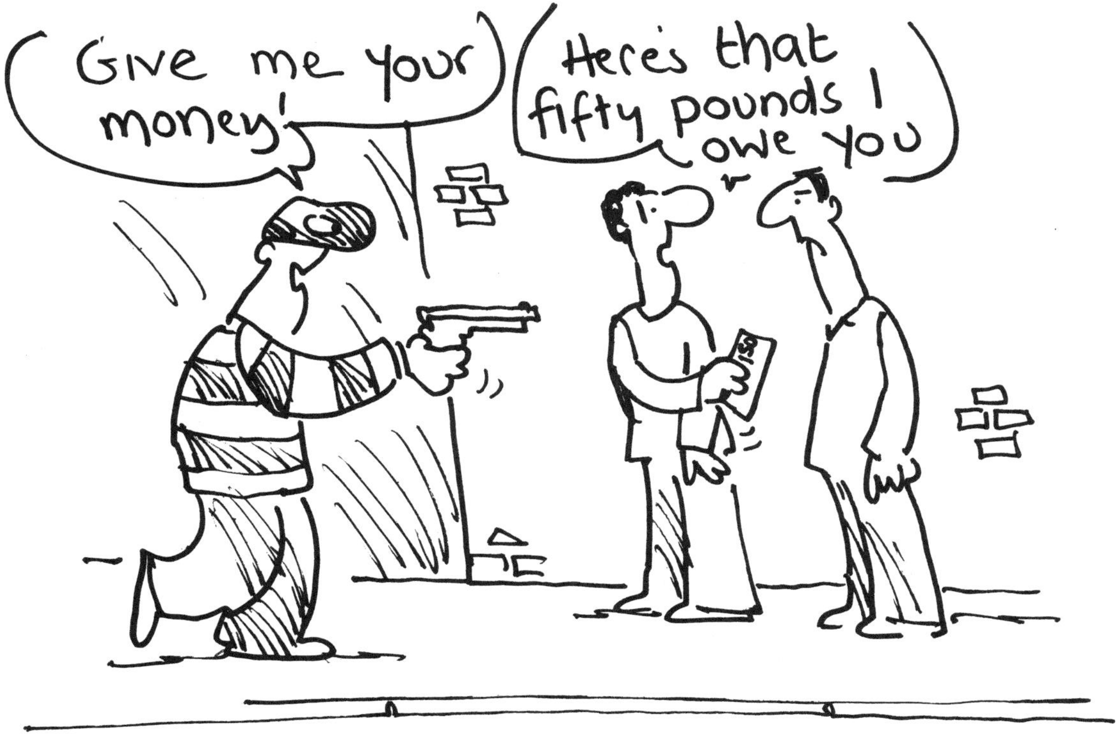
Give me your money!
Here's that fifty pounds I owe you

What's a cow's favourite musical?

Answer – The Sound of Mooosic.

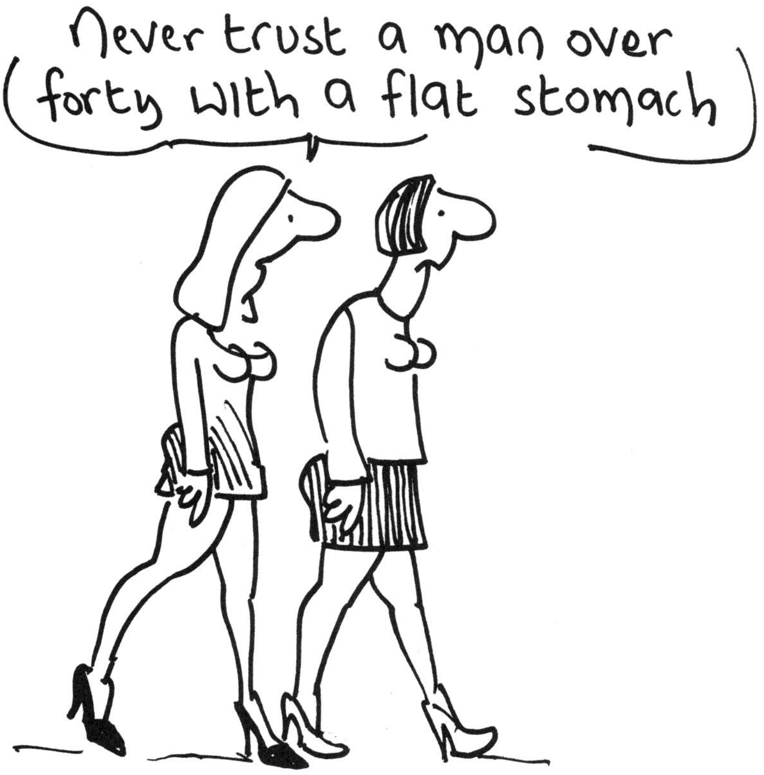
Never trust a man over forty with a flat stomach

Where do sheep drink?

Answer – Baaaars.

Why do women have orgasms?

Answer – It's just another excuse to moan.

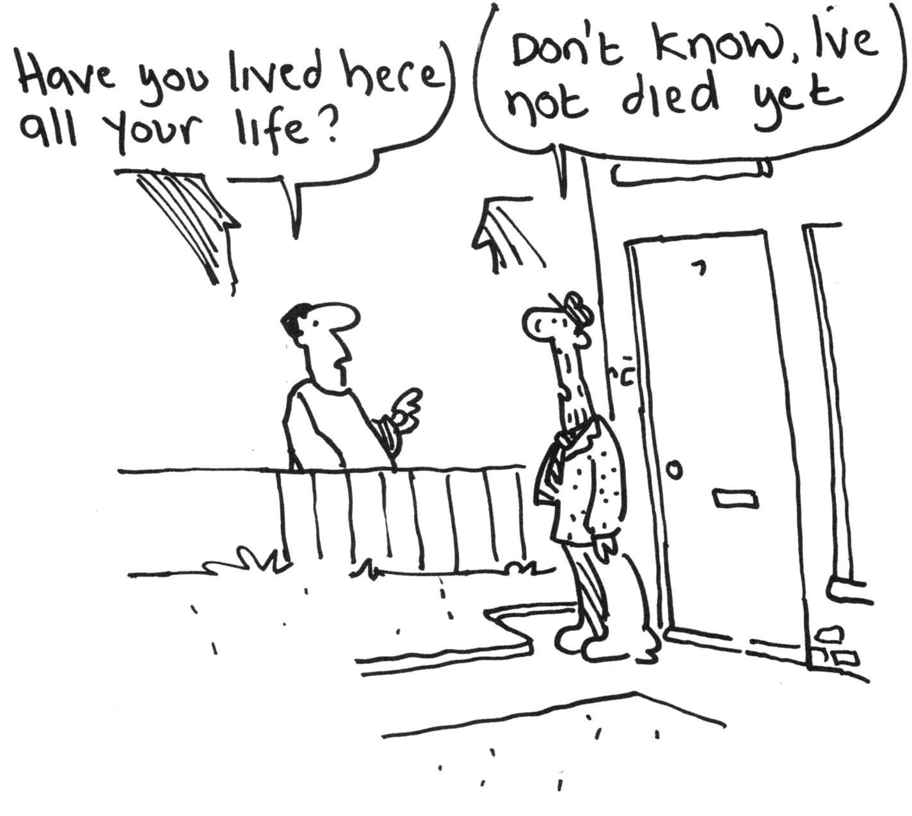
Have you lived here all your life?
Don't know, I've not died yet

Two goldfish are in their tank.
One turns to the other and says,
'You man the guns, I'll drive.'

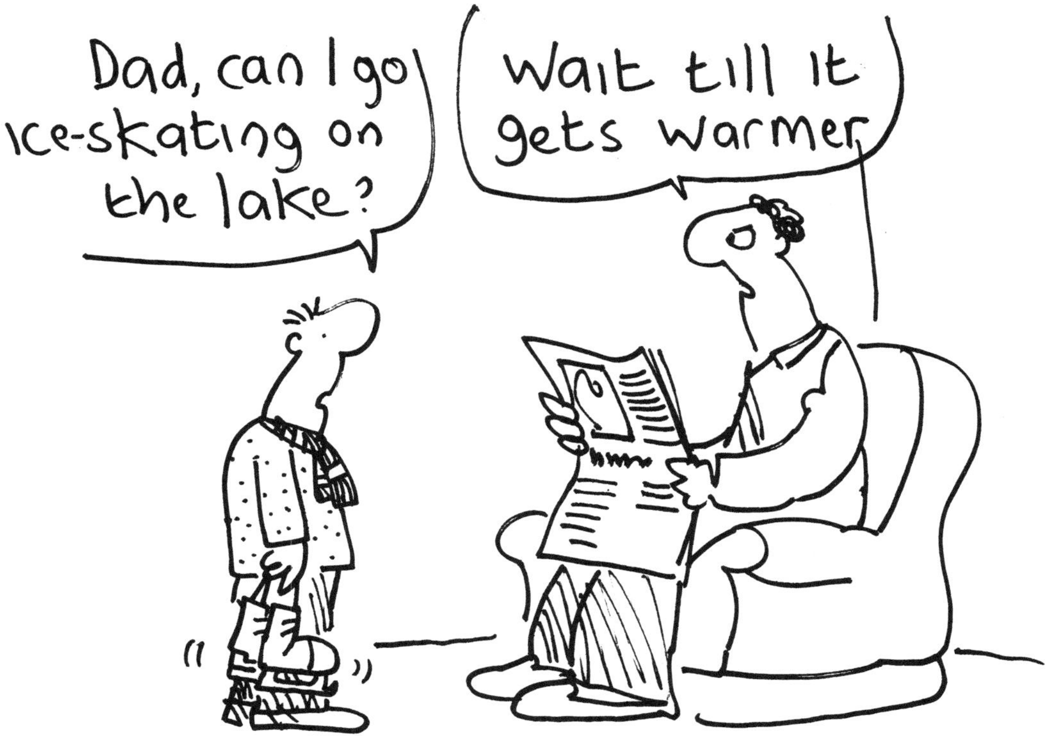
Dad, can I go ice-skating on the lake?
Wait till it gets warmer

My sister had a baby, so I went round to see her. She said, 'Would you mind winding him for me?' So I thumped him in the stomach.

I was a fool when I married you!
I know, but I was in love and didn't notice

Little Johnny was born a perfectly normal, healthy baby, except for the fact that he was just a head. No arms, no legs, no torso – nothing. Just a head.

Amazingly he led a perfectly happy life for the first few years, until he started school and the other kids started to tease him about his disability. So, as a special treat for his seventh birthday, Mum and Dad bought him a ticket to Disneyland.

When the special morning arrived, Mum and Dad crept up to his bedroom, knocked on the door and shouted, 'Surprise!'

'Don't tell me,' thought Johnny wearily. 'Another bloody hat!'

There are three things that happen when you get to my age, first your memory goes and...I've forgotten the other two

A man with a big orange head walks into a bar and orders a drink. While the barman is pouring a drink he looks at the man and says, 'I hope you don't mind me asking, but what's with the big orange head?' The man replies, 'It's a strange story: I was in the woods and came across a fairy who granted me three wishes. My first wish was for a million pound a week and she granted me that; my second wish was a fleet of Rolls Royces, which she granted; and the third, for some stupid reason, I asked for a big orange head!'

What do you put on your rhubarb?
Horse manure, usually
Oooh... we put custard on ours

My great uncle died at the Battle of the Little Big Horn. He wasn't fighting there but he'd been camping in the next field and went over to complain about the noise.

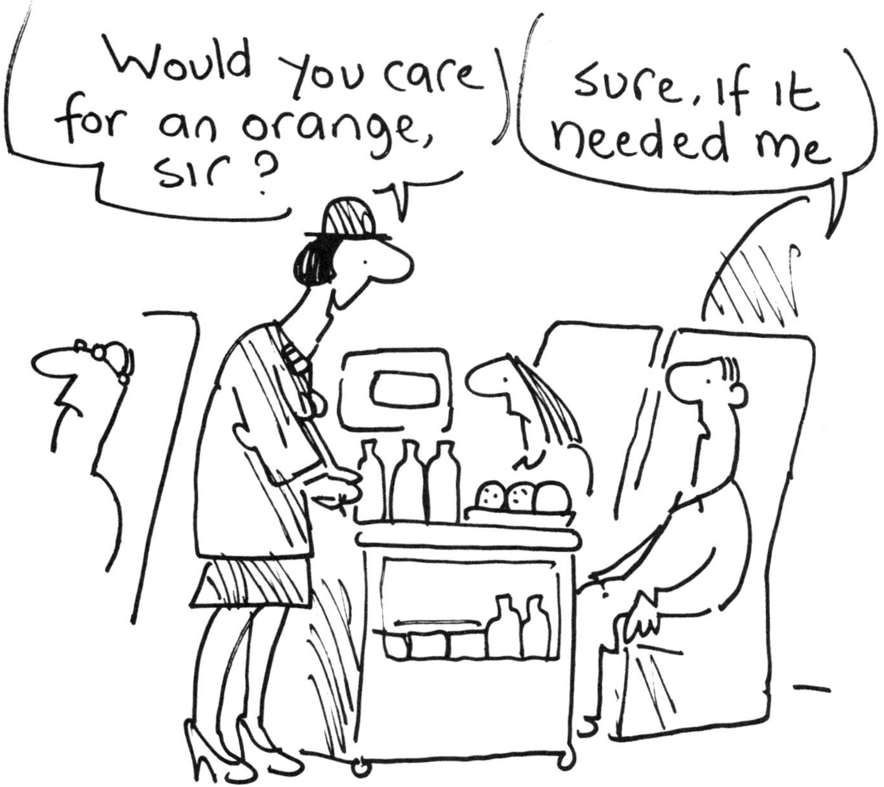
Would you care for an orange, sir?
Sure, if it needed me

Two men in a bar. The first says, 'My friend's wife has divorced her husband for snoring.' The second man replies, 'I didn't think you could get divorced for snoring.' The first man says, 'Well, he's a ventriloquist and he snored on her side of the bed.'

What did you learn at school today?
Not enough apparently, Ive got to go back tomorrow

Two lions escape from London Zoo.
As they are walking through Trafalgar Square
one says to the other, 'You'd think there'd be
more people about, wouldn't you?'

Why do you want this book?
'cause I collect moths
BOOKSTORE
ADVICE FOR YOUNG MOTHERS

Two soldiers are at the side of Culloden Field, waiting for the battle to commence. One says to the other, 'I could murder a McDonald's!'

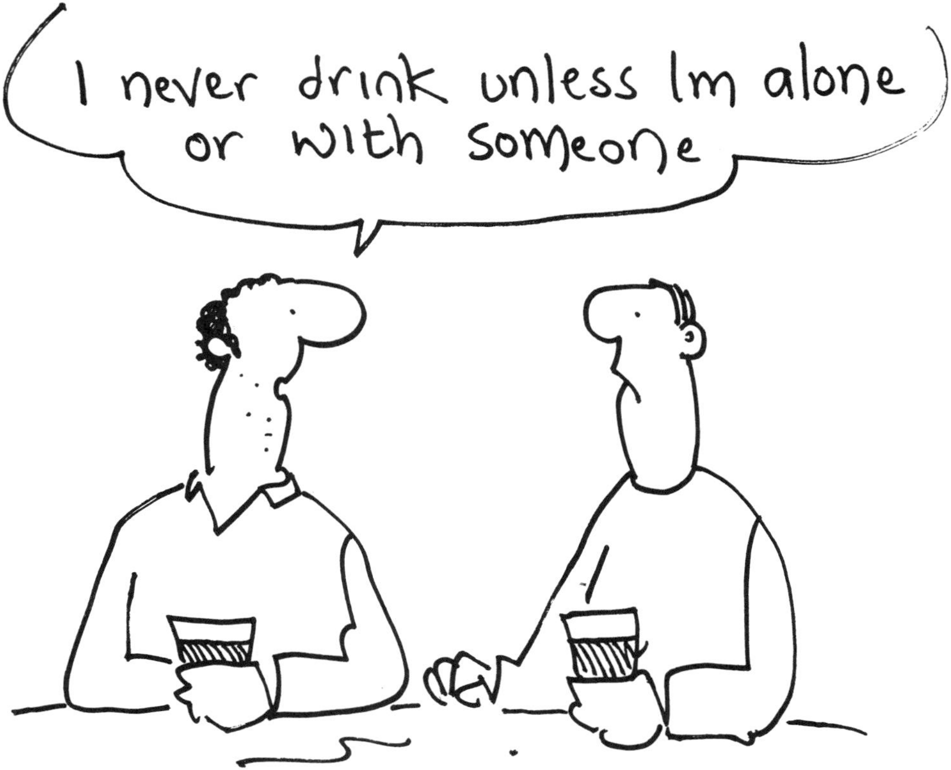
I never drink unless Im alone or with someone

How many psychologists does it take to change a light bulb?

Just one, but the light bulb has to want to change.

Mr Smith, I want Your daughter for my wife
Well go home and tell Your wife she can't have my daughter!

What's the difference between snowmen and snow-women?

Snowballs.

Which are the men and which are the women?
I Don't know, they're not wearing any clothes
NUDIST CAMP

A woman walks into a bar and asks the barman for a double entendre, so the barman gives her one.

A boat carrying red paint and a boat carrying blue paint have collided. Apparently the crew were Marooned
NEWS

What's red and invisible?

No tomatoes.

I'm going to make you the happiest woman in the world
I'll miss you

What does a man with two left feet wear?

Flip-flips.

Who'd want to live to be 100?!
Someone who's 99
Man celebrates 100th birthday

An Englishman, an Irishman and an American arrive on the viewing deck of the Empire State Building. The American stands on the parapet and says, 'I'm going to fly around New York and then land back here.' He takes off, flies around New York and then lands safely back where he started. The Irishman climbs up on the parapet and says, 'Right, I'll do the same.' He leaps off the edge and plummets to his death. The Englishman turns to the American and says, 'Bleedin'ell, you're a bastard when you're pissed, Superman!'

There was a snake on my windscreen this morning
Really?!
Yes, it was a windscreen viper

How many surrealists does it take to change a light bulb?

Fish.

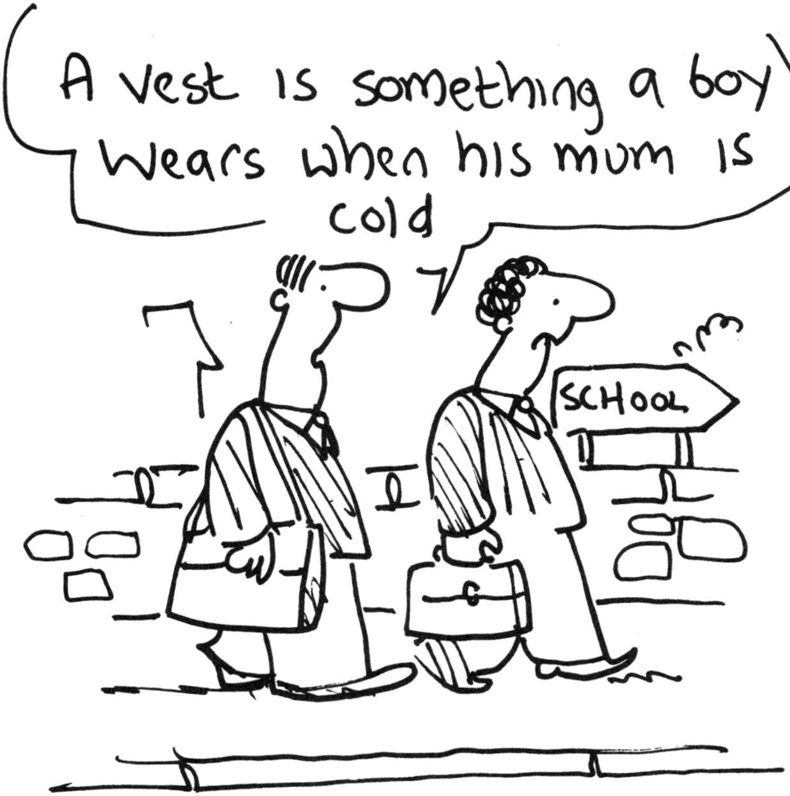
A vest is something a boy wears when his mum is cold
SCHOOL

What did the cow say to the farmer?

You never kiss me when you're playing with my tits.

Mum, would you like to be cremated or buried?
I don't know, surprise me

A truck driver is delivering some penguins to a zoo in a refrigerated truck. The truck breaks down and the penguins start to overheat, so he flags down another refrigerated truck.

Driver: 'If I give you £50 will you take these penguins to the zoo?'

Second driver: 'Sure, load them in the back.' They do and he drives off.

Hours later the truck has been repaired and the first driver is driving through the town when he sees the second driver leading the penguins down the street. He pulls over. Driver: 'What are you doing?

Second driver: 'Well I took them to the zoo and I've got some change from the £50, so I'm taking them to the pictures.'

Have you heard the one about the dyslexic, insomniac and agnostic who stayed awake all night wondering if there was a dog?

We don't get many polar bears in here
At these prices I'm not surprised
WINE BAR

First man – I just heard an extraordinary thing.

Second man – What's that?

First man – Every time I breath, a man dies.

Second man – Oh dear. You want to try chewing cloves.

id like something tall, icy and full of vodka
Joanne, it's for you

What do you do if a bird craps on your windscreen?

Finish with her.

Doctor, I keeping thinking I'm a packet of savoury biscuits
Oh dear, you must be crackers
DOCTOR

Two girls in a bar. One says to the other, 'I've had sex in 110 posistions.' The second girl replies, '110? I didn't know there were that many. Let's just go through them: there's the missionary position ...' The first girl interrupts, 'Oh yeah, sorry, I meant 111 positions.'

How dare you fart in front of my wife!
Sorry, I didn't realise it was her turn

Two men in a bar.
First man – Who's your tailor?
Second man – Why?
First man – That was my second question.

Three weeks ago my wife learned to drive. Last week she learned to aim it

I once bought my kids a set of batteries for Christmas with a note on it saying toys not included.

You know if I was 2" bigger I'd be a King!
..and if you were 2" smaller you'd be a queen

Have you heard about the Irishman who reversed into a car-boot sale and sold the engine?

The early bird catches the worm!
Yeah, but the second mouse gets the cheese

So I rang up British Telecom and said, 'I want to report a nuisance caller.' He said, 'Not you again.'

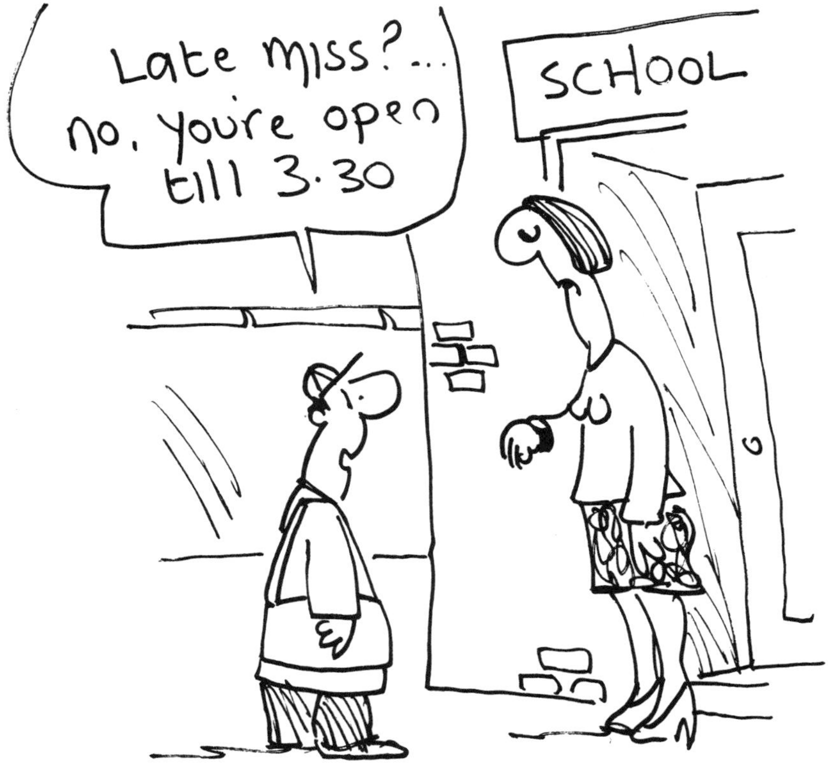
Late miss?... no, you're open till 3.30
SCHOOL

'Mummy, mummy, can I lick the bowl?'

'No, you can flush it like everyone else!'

Why didn't You put an advert in the paper when Your dog got lost?
er... 'cause it can't read

What was E.T. short for?

Because he had little legs.

Paddy and Mick are walking along when suddenly Paddy falls down a hole.

Paddy: 'Jesus, this hole's got milk in it!'

Mick: 'Is it pasteurised?'

Paddy: 'No it's just up to my ankles.'

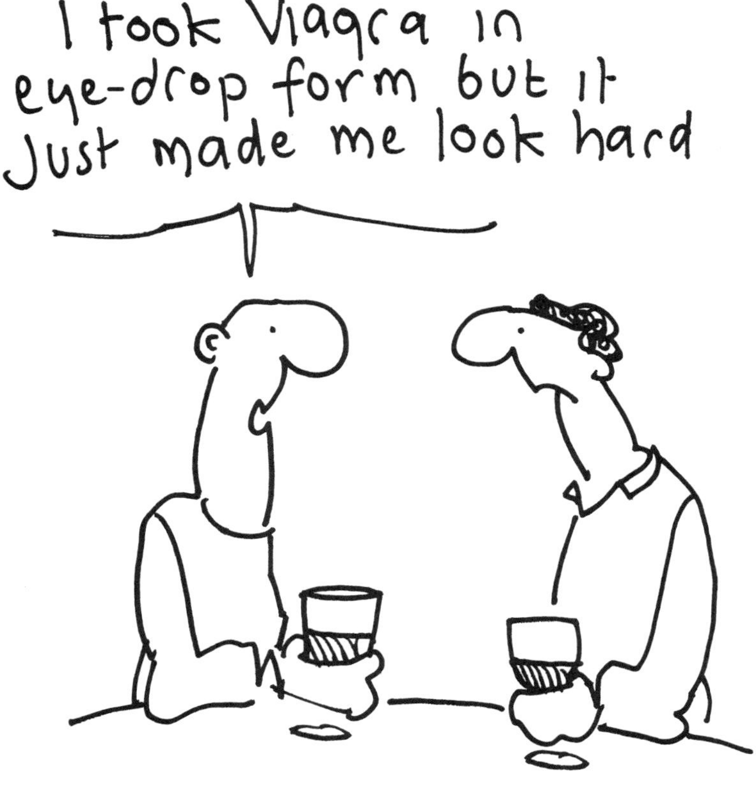
I took Viagra in eye-drop form but it just made me look hard

A band are rehearsing when the guitarist's string breaks. They send the drummer out to get some new strings. He goes into the shop and asks the assistant if he can buy some. The assistant says, 'You're a drummer, aren't you?'

'Yes,' replies the drummer, 'how did you guess?'

'This is a chip shop, mate.'

Whats the best way of contacting long-lost relatives?
Win the lottery
CITIZENS ADVICE

A little balloon goes to his mum and dad in bed. He asks if he can get in with them. Dad says no and sends him back to his own bed. Later the little balloon goes back to his mum and dad's bed. They're asleep so he tries to get in bed with them, but there is no room so he lets some air out of his mum and some air out of his dad. Again he tries to get in bed with them, but still there is no room. So he lets some air out of himself. This time there is room and he snuggles between them and goes to sleep. Next morning he is woken by his dad, furious at seeing the little balloon in bed with them. His dad shouts: I'm very annoyed. You've let me down, you've let your mum down but, more importantly, you've let yourself down!

mmm ... I see what's wrong with you. You're not eating properly
DOCTOR

Napoleon is leading his army to Moscow. At the brow of a hill he holds up his arm and shouts: 'Halt.'

The army of some 200,000 grinds to a halt. From the back, one soldier breaks free and runs past all his fellow soldiers. After ten minutes he reaches Napoleon and stands in front of him. Napoleon looks him up and down and says: 'Yes?'

The soldier looks at him and says: 'I thought you shouted Walt.'

Batman? ... Naw, he's Just gone for a batpiss

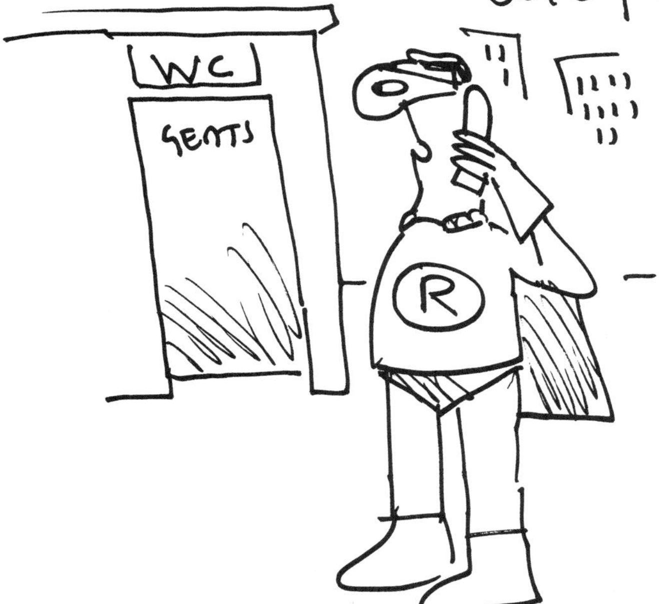